Blow His Mind

Her Illustrated Guide to Sensational Oral Sex, Give him the Best Blow Job of His Life! Master Advanced Fellatio Tonight

Melinda Holmes

PUBLISHING

Atlanta, Georgia USA

ISBN 978-1-491010-57-0

9 781491 010570 >

Readers' Testimonials

"Being a sensual being is nothing to feel ashamed of anymore. And I am so glad that more books come out all the time exploring our sexuality. This is one of the best out there."

★★★★☆**Olga C. Jackson, Illinois**

"Sometimes it does take a book to help you learn a lot of things that have to do with the experience of sex. I never was a big fan of guides but this one has proved really useful to me, so I'm more than grateful for discovering it."

★★★★★**Molly S. Bowling, New York**

"I'd recommend this book to anyone who likes to experiment in their sex life. It offers some food for thought and, as expected, lots of pleasure as well."

★★★★★**Barbara D. Chou, Las Vegas**

Exclusive Bonus Download: 101 Steps To A Happy Relationship

Dating and marriage is different today than it was twenty years ago. In today's society, more than 50% of all marriages fail for one reason or another. Just thinking about that makes "commitment" seem scary. It seems that when relationships are faced with challenges, people quit trying.

The fact is that relationships, whether dating or married, are hard. Things do not always go perfectly, fighting does occur, and it takes a 100% commitment from both parties to make it a success.

There are hundreds of things you can do to better your relationship. To help get you headed in the right direction, 101 Steps To A Happy Relationship

<u>**Download this guide and start improving your relationship NOW**</u>

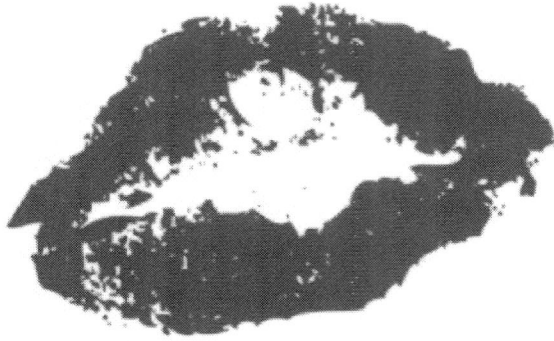

Thank you for downloading my book. Please REVIEW this book on Amazon. I need your feedback to make the next version better. Thank you so much!

Author's Foreword

I know that this guide will come as a surprise to many and perhaps that's one of the reasons that I wrote it. Fellatio is one of the most important parts of lovemaking so mastering some new techniques and thus offering more pleasure to your man can prove of great value, something that would add some spice to your life and that would also make you enjoy a more adventurous and colorful relationship.

Men like to be taken care of, everybody knows that. And everybody knows that a good blowjob can go a long way when it comes to keeping desire to the maximum. It doesn't matter how sensual a person is or isn't; what matters is that they don't spare any time or effort to offer pleasure to their partner.

Sex comes bearing gifts and asks of them as well, so every time you give something to your partner you obviously expect to receive something in return. Mastering the art of fellatio doesn't seem to be an easy thing to do to a lot of women, but that doesn't mean that it's difficult or that they shouldn't try it. This guide will help them understand it better and it will open their eyes to new sexual and sensual possibilities.

TABLE OF CONTENTS

Disclaimer

Introduction

"Take my word for it, it doesn't bite," Alec said.

"But, it's the thing you pee out of," I whined.

"Yes," he conceded. *"But I won't be peeing out of it now."* His logic reassured me only a little in persuading me to give him a blow job, or as I would have called it at the time, 'an act of fellatio.'

Nonetheless, we settled down to the act, and although unsatisfactory, my boyfriend Alec received a passable blow job, and he came, in my mouth – which pleased him, but at the time, grossed me out.

Since that time, I've known a few more men during my research as an erotic writer. Some of those men were just nice guys I've met, some were in the adult film industry, and some, believe it or not, were purely for research. Each of the ones that I may mention in the guide involved my taking his penis in my mouth, and bringing him to a high level of excitement, then taking the consequences. Which, when you get right down to it, summarizes the basic components of fellatio, also known as "sucking cock," "a blow job," and "a hummer," among other slang names.

I guess that I've come a good distance from my upbringing as a Catholic school girl in California – though what they say about some of us ("Blow Job Specialists") is possibly true, somehow I missed that club in high school. Since that time, I've learned an awful lot from men that I've played with, from many gay men, and even from other women. I've been in threesomes – some with other women, which enabled me to learn from watching how they handled the man, and some with two men, which gave me the opportunity to multi-task men, and even watch how one man blows another man.

1

All of those situations taught me important things to keep in mind in regard to a woman giving a man a *satisfactory* blow job. Anyone can suck a dick, but not many can give their man complete and total satisfaction – the kind of bliss that ensures he won't stray, at least because of your sexual ability!

This guide is intended to teach you all that you need to know (or want to know) about sucking a dick successfully, and leaving behind a shaken shell of a man who has just experienced a blow job that he Never. Will. Forget.

And more importantly, the techniques and positions you will learn here will give you the confidence to help you develop a better position within an existing relationship, and stimulate his devotion to you, making you into the goddess that every man secretly desires and aches to worship!

Fellatio, Blow Job, Cock Sucking – What's in a Name?

Throughout the course of this guide I'm going to refer to our subject as "fellatio," with the occasional lapse into more colorful terms. Men often use terms like "blow job," "cock sucking," or "giving head," as both descriptions to identify the act (which I do not mind), but also sometimes as derogatory terms, or as insults to demean women. That always annoys me, as a well performed blow job can be a man's brief visit to paradise – you would think that they'd have a little more respect for an act of sharing with that much power over them! Believe me, I have NO compunctions about getting filthy and dirty in describing sex – the dirtier the better, since I'm a writer of erotica after all - but I'd like to leave the insulting implications out.

Frankly, any man should be thrilled that someone wants to bring him to climax using their mouth, right? I know I'm pretty happy when someone licks my pussy and clit! So, let's talk about just what constitutes fellatio...

"Fellatio is an act of oral stimulation of the penis by a sexual partner... It involves the stimulation of the penis by the use of the mouth, lips, tongue or throat... Fellatio is regarded by many as an erotic act in its own right and a physically intimate act. For many males, it is a turn-on which may be used by the giving partner to initiate foreplay and sexual arousal before sexual intercourse. The act may also be performed for the sexual gratification derived by the male receiving partner and can be continued until orgasm and ejaculation of semen..." - Wikipedia

At its basics, fellatio consists of someone putting their mouth around someone else's penis. The difference between an unforgettable act of fellatio, and a very forgettable one, are all the little tips and techniques that a smart, interested, and sexy woman brings to bear, versus a woman who just wants to get things over with. With fellatio, a little investment in learning on your part can pay big dividends!

"My sister, of all people, swore that learning to suck a man's cock correctly could make him your slave for life. To my surprise, I've found that to be essentially true. Though I've made some mistakes in the types of men that I've become interested in, I've never had any difficulty in persuading them to listen to me about virtually anything important. I kind of thought it was something like the way men listen to a baseball player tell them which car they should buy. A man's respect for authority can lead him to some strange sources, I guess." – Beth, 35

Becoming a Fellatio Goddess

It's the heat, moisture, friction, AND "pressure differential" of a woman's mouth that make a great blow job so memorable, since all four contribute to the physical stimulation of the thousands of nerve endings in a man's penis, as well as the various mental stimuli involved in a memorable blow job.

Besides the surface texture issues, there is the ability to change the pressure around the man's cock, the "pressure differential." A 'blow job' doesn't normally involve 'blowing' at all. It's more of a slight sucking with the girl's mouth. Just gentle, slight sucking – you don't need to pull his semen out, it's perfectly capable of coming out on its own! It's just a nice little, extra touch which differentiates the memorable blow job from a completely forgettable waste of time.

And of course there are your lips, gums, and especially the tongue, which can bring in a whole extra set of textural sensations to please the man, and excite his cock.

Just as your pussy is more than simply a place for him to dump semen, so is your mouth a source of pleasurable sensation during the memorable blow job. But even beyond the above-mentioned sources of his pleasure, there's yet more!

You can (and should) be stroking his cock with the fingertips of one hand, while your mouth is busy on the so-so-sensitive head. And your other hand? There's the underside of his thighs, his ball sack, or scrotum, and if you and your man have an understanding.... his asshole!

Yes, men often shoot immediately when their anal sphincter is played with, lightly. Some men will go for having your finger penetrate them, essentially getting off on being finger fucked while they fuck your mouth. Stimulating the prostate inside a man's body with a finger, penis or similar object is a long-recognized source of immense, intense pleasure among gay men.

Keep in mind, though, that you need LOTS of lube to slide your finger up his ass, and some men are going to have a little 'gay phobia' thing going with hard, pointy things in their anus, so either your man needs to be pretty wild and accepting, or you should really bring it up in conversation beforehand.

Compare that to the unsatisfactory fellatio that men complain about (and they DO, endlessly!)

"Sheila was the worst cock sucker. She'd put her mouth on my cock alright, but that was it... well, fuck, when I'm fucking her, I don't just stick my dick in her pussy and lay there, right? She moves so sweetly, her hips rotating around, even her pussy squeezing me, that it's always fun. But blow jobs? She was a dead fish, frankly.

When I couldn't get her to do a little more, it just annoyed me, and I guess it snowballed from there. I started seeing Annie. She's something else with her mouth, AND she's pretty open to a lot of other things, too." – Mike, 23

There's no question that "Mike" is a shallow, immature asshole, and Sheila's probably better off without him in the long run, but really, why alienate your man, when pleasing him is so easy? Sheila could add just a little to her cock sucking technique, and hold on to the next, presumably nicer, guy she's attracted to. Even better, maybe she'll simply move up to a nicer *class* of guy!

There are adult erotic movies available called "POV" videos, short for "point of view." They're basically taken from the man's perspective as if he were watching the woman "perform" for him, i.e., looking down

6

at her as she performs fellatio. They're wildly popular, because men really get off watching a woman take the presumably submissive position of sucking his cock. And when the woman looks up at him with an expression of desire in her eyes, he's guaranteed to get off, and quickly. It's kind of a 'power' thing, although in reality, as with all dominant and submissive couplings, the power actually resides with the submissive partner. In the case of a straight couple's blow job, that's the female.

Putting Fellatio on the Menu

Please keep in mind that men are less interested in foreplay than women are. They are much more easily brought to a peak of anticipation and pleasure, and so, where cunnilingus for women will be a part of the emotional experience of making love (or just having sex), fellatio may be the entire thing for a man.

You probably might want to make fellatio an event that's "special." By that, I mean you don't want to agree to give him head whenever you go to bed, at least not to completion, because if he climaxes, as you probably know by now, he's finished for the night. So use fellatio as a teasing part of your play, to get him excited, but not to cause him to climax – unless that's your goal.

Blow him to get him excited and ready for fucking, blow him to get him to come, but make sure that's what you want. If he shoots his wad (comes) in your mouth, and you were expecting to fuck, I'm sorry, but that long, delicious fuck is not going to happen, no matter how mad you get.

Variation in the little "extras" that you incorporate into your fellatio technique will make it fresh and new for him each time, and consequently enable you to bring him to the desired point of excitement. Lightly fondling his balls, stroking the underside of his thighs, playing with his asshole, gazing up at him with clear desire in your eyes – each of these will take his penis from "6 o'clock to midnight" in just a few seconds – but not if you do the same thing every time.

Mix it up!

Tantric sex and "good" teasing

A man's immediate urge when having sex, is to come as quickly as possible. What some men have come to realize, is that putting off that orgasm can extend his pleasure and yours, a truly win-win situation. It takes some practice and time, but learning to slowly bring a man to the peak of orgasm with your mouth, then backing off it, allows him to 'cool down' a bit and prevents ejaculation. This allows him to enjoy the sensations brought about by a near-orgasm, without the subsequent loss of interest that invariably results when he does finally come.

This concept is widely practiced as "tantric sex," "orgasm control," or "edging," and is favored by individuals and partners interested in prolonging and extending the pleasure of orgasm far beyond the simple climax that most people accept.

It's the movement and contact of skin against his cock, balls, thighs, and anal area that excite him the most as he approaches orgasm. Lessening that contact and movement will either slow or stop the increase in his excitement, and prevent his ejaculation and subsequent loss of interest in continuing.

It usually isn't necessary to completely abandon touching or mouthing him, as that would likely be upsetting. Simply stop or slow the movement of your lips, mouth, or tongue on his cock, and your fingers on the shaft of his cock or elsewhere on his previously mentioned erogenous areas. Transfer your fingertip stroking to other, less sensitive areas like his stomach, chest, arms, and lower legs – he may not even notice that you're slowing down his excitement!

Eventually, with his help and cooperation, you can get him to the point where he experiences multiple orgasms. For men, that is a very memorable experience! And there's a side benefit for women whose men may experience premature ejaculation. This kind of training can help prevent that disappointment, allowing the man to orgasm when you both desire it.

Be an Olympic Gold Medal Winner in Fellatio

What is the secret of giving an "Olympic Gold Medal" Blow Job? Simply, it's a matter of giving the man more sensations than just a mouth on a cock. It's a matter of giving him pleasurable sensations in several areas at once, while keeping the main focus on his cock, and varying those sensations during the act of fellatio. In this guide, you will learn about many different techniques in giving head, sucking cock, giving a blow job, in becoming a goddess of fellatio for your man. Be that winner!

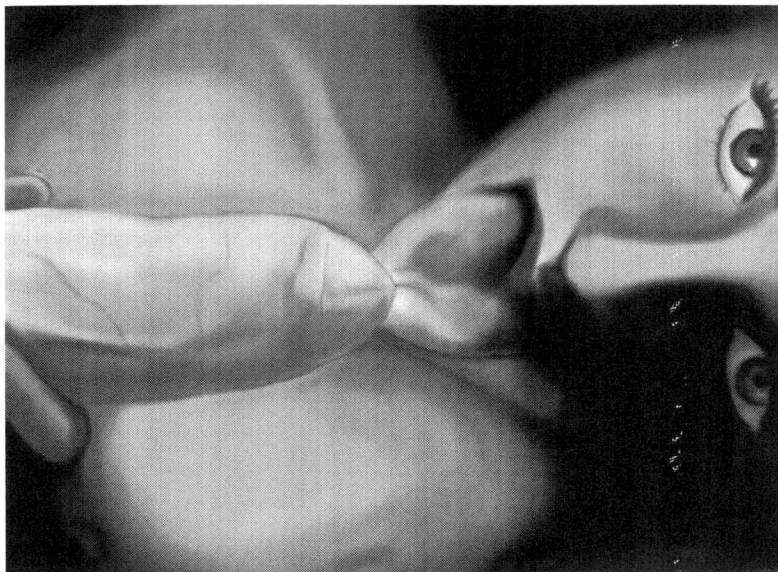

Fellatio and Men's Anatomy

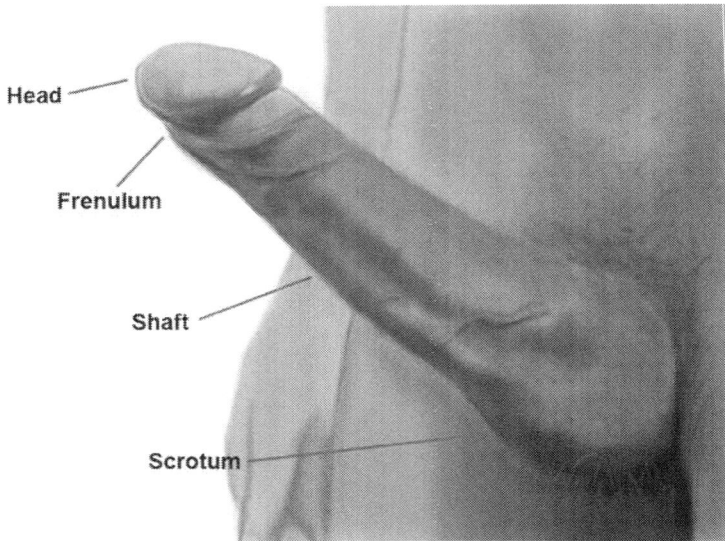

Head

Frenulum

Shaft

Scrotum

Cock Head

Commonly, the first place on the penis that your lips will contact during fellatio, is the head. This is also known as the "glans," and most likely is the source of the expression "giving head." This portion of the penis is the closest equivalent in a man to a woman's clitoris, although it only has about a third of the nerve endings that are found in the clitoris, which accounts for the fact that it can be handled a little more vigorously than the clit. It's a great area to bring pleasurable stimulation to your man, and indicates how important the action of your tongue, lips, and mouth are to him during fellatio, as most women can't effectively take in much more than the head when the penis is erect.

Frenulum

The frenulum is the spot on the underside of the penis, where the head joins the shaft. This is probably the second-richest area on the circumcised penis for nerve endings, and licking, kissing, stroking, rubbing, and caressing of this area will usually reward a woman with positive reactions from her male partner.

Shaft

The shaft of the penis gets all the notice, as everyone - but especially males themselves - comments at some point on a man's "size," and it's the shaft which contributes the most to that commentary. It's debatable how important the length or the girth of the penis actually is, but it certainly makes a difference to couples interested in "deep throating," which is the woman's ability to take the full length of the penis into her mouth and upper throat. As the shaft has relatively few nerve endings, this area may contribute much less than the head, frenulum, foreskin, and even testicles to either the man's satisfaction or the woman's ability to bring him to climax through fellatio.

This area probably benefits most from soft, caressing contact with a woman's fingers and palm stroking his shaft, while her lips, mouth, and tongue are stimulating his far more sensitive head, foreskin (if present), and frenulum.

Scrotum

Unfortunately for the male, the scrotum-- the fleshy sack containing his testicles (aka "balls," "stones,", "bollocks"), does not contribute as much sensation of pleasure to the man as either the head or frenulum, as they do the potential for pain if hit or abused, or even handled the least bit too roughly. In that sense, they are equivalent to the clitoris as a source of pain. While they don't often contribute heavily to a male's arousal, still soft, gentle caressing, cupping, kissing and mouthing of the scrotum does feel pleasurable to a man and is usually appreciated during fellatio.

Circumcised versus Uncircumcised

When a male is born, he has a piece of skin attached to the head of his penis, called the 'foreskin.' This piece protects the sensitive head of the penis from over stimulation, as the clitoral hood protects the clitoris. And just as in the clitoral hood, the foreskin also has numerous nerve endings, and can be a significant source of pleasure. However, for various reasons, legitimate or not, today, in many societies and cultures the foreskin is removed in the act called "circumcision." So, a circumcised male will be missing this foreskin,

15

and the head of his penis will be exposed at all times, while the penis of the uncircumcised male will usually be covered by it, other than when his penis is erect and extended, pulling the foreskin back from the head.

This can present more opportunities for a woman to pleasure the uncircumcised male than in the circumcised. Stroking, kissing, licking, and just manipulation of the foreskin will send a bevy of pleasurable sensations throughout the man's groin. Enjoy whichever a man offers to you – since most circumcisions are done at a very early age, chances are that he had no choice in the matter!

Preparation for Fellatio

In order to make fellatio enjoyable for both partners, it's beneficial to "prepare the field" for play. A clean cock is a tasty cock, but don't let your man neglect other areas as well.

Showering

Contrary to rumors and gossip, generally speaking, a man's scent after a hard day at work is a little more difficult to take than a woman's. Perhaps it's the result of out of control pheromones, body bacteria, or just because men sometimes aren't as careful about routine hygiene as women. I'd much rather lick another woman's pussy as my after work cocktail, than suck a dick – if hygiene is a significant factor. Regardless, oral sex is almost always better after a shower, if the recipient of your oral loving has been generating sweat for some long period of time. The pleasant aroma of fresh sweat is quickly converted to less pleasant odors over time.

The best way to get to that point is to suggest a shower together – after all, if you've been working, you might not be the freshest thing to attract his oral attention either! And while you're in there, why not stroke that hot, fat cock of his to get him ready for your mouth? And whether you do it, or he does it, make sure his backside gets thoroughly scrubbed, too. Nothing destroys the mood like stray scents from that area, when neglected.

Shaving

Pubic hair tends to hold onto odors – those last few drops of his pee that he has trouble shaking off, the thin coating of sweat that generates quickly in his crotch, "Klingons" in his anal area – yuck! The less hair, the better, these days, it seems. If he hasn't gotten with current trends, you can suggest it to him. Here are some advantages of removing some or all of his hair down there:

- **Stay cool.** Hair is insulation that holds in body heat – hot crotch happens when he's got a fur coat down there. He can stay cooler, and develop less embarrassing, and smelly, crotch sweat. He doesn't need to go completely bald, just thinning and shortening the forest will be a big improvement.
- **Go big or go home.** A thinned out pubic thatch emphasizes his cock, instead of it being lost in the forest of fur. Cocks look a lot bigger when they're not competing with his bush. Tell him how attractive his penis and scrotum are, and how you'd love an unobstructed view, especially when that view is likely to draw your mouth down there. Then get out of his way as he races to the bathroom to trim it!
- **Easy means more often.** Men's groins are easier to maintain, and less prone to miscellaneous minor disasters, when his bush is nonexistent or at least trimmed. Plus, he's more in tune with current fashion. And getting his ass trimmed isn't such a bad idea either. If you're one of the women into analingus, it makes that particular endeavor loads more fun.

When shaving your man, keep these things in mind:

- Use scissors to do the preliminary underbrush trimming.
- Use single or double edge disposable razors – they're cheaper to replace than the multiple blade regular cartridges, and pubic hair is rough on blade life.
- How about a romantic soaking bath together, to soften his pubic bush, and get you both in the mood for lots of lovin'?
- If you don't have time for that bath, try conditioner on his bush – let it soak for a few minutes before continuing.
- Volunteer to help him shave, of course. He'll appreciate the assistance, or even better, you taking over the shaving duties. Plus, there's no man alive who doesn't like the feel of someone's attentive fingers on his crotch!

- Cortisone creams or cornstarch can help with minor irritations.
- It's probably safer to use unscented, dye free soap, shaving cream and skin lotions. This is no time to discover allergen sensitivities.

Waxing

Most men have to be talked into a waxing, especially if they've seen *"The 40 Year Old Virgin,"* which has a horrific waxing scene. You'll have to judge whether it's worth the effort with your man, although some men have no problem at all with it. If a man does go through with it, the results are great — hair stays away much longer than with shaving, and returning hair is thinner and less of an issue.

Do be honest with him. There IS pain, but it goes away pretty quickly. Also, if he's prone to ingrown hairs, that also can be a problem with waxing.

Giving Your Man the Greatest Pleasure

Putting Him in Sexual Hyperdrive

The most active sense of the 5 senses for men sexually, is vision. Men react very quickly, and very strongly, to what they can see – the entire adult film industry is built on that reaction. And while much of fellatio is perceived through touch, nonetheless, what the man sees can be decisive in whether he sees you as a sexual "goddess," or a sexual "dud-ess."

You may already know that men react very strongly to depictions of female body parts. The sight of a woman's bum, or breasts, apart from their being a part of the whole, is extremely exciting to men. Yes, you can call it demeaning, or dehumanizing, but the fact of the matter is, as a lawyer would say, *res ipsa loquitor*, or, "the thing speaks for itself." Men have no control over that response, so you might as well use it for your own purposes, and recognize that simply showing him certain parts of your body in a sexy way will flip his switch.

Another thing that you might NOT know, is that men are wildly turned on by seeing a woman undergoing intense sexual pleasure, as evidenced by "gasping, moaning, screaming, and swooning," as Leon Seltzer, Ph. D explained in his article, "*Evolution of the Self – The Triggers of Sexual Desire*" in **Psychology Today (May 11, 2012.)** So why not outwardly express the sexual pleasure that you'd like to be experiencing, if it leads to your man becoming instantly electrified with desire for you? Moan, sigh, coo with pleasure as you suck his cock, play with yourself – yes, rub your clit, rock your hips, pinch your nipples, get flushed with desire – if you're not going to get excited and show it, why should he?

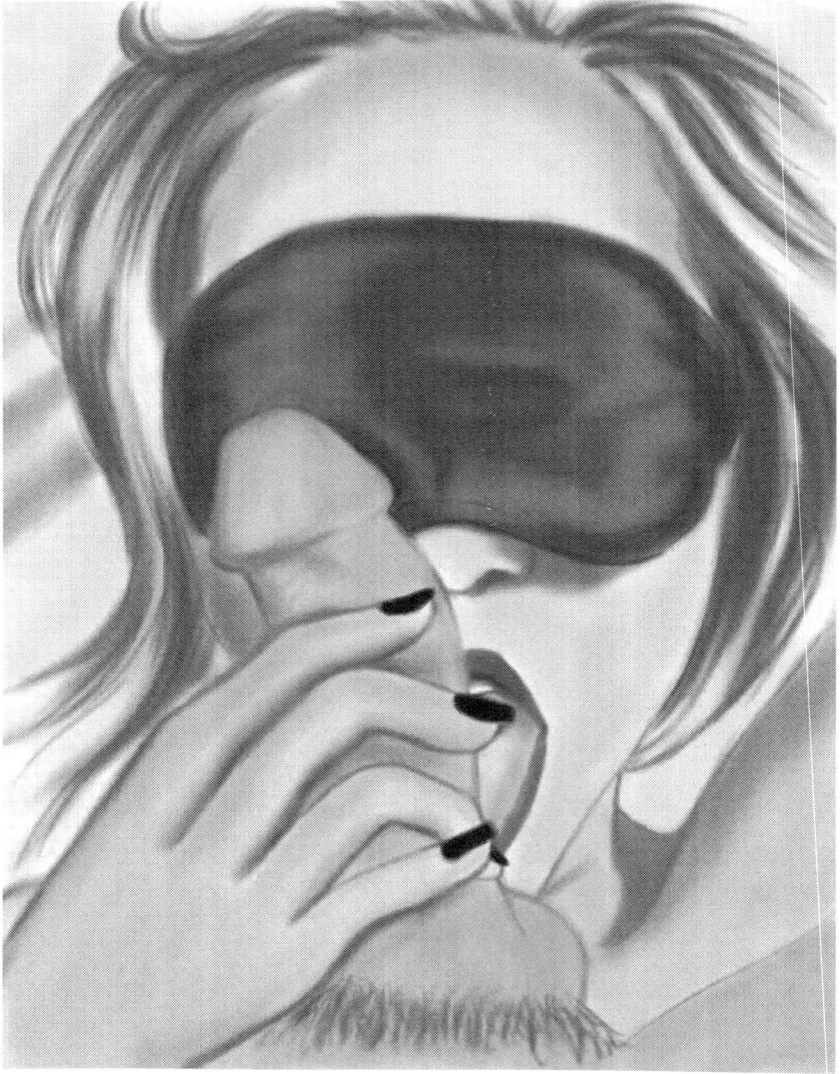

Own the Moment - Keep These Things in Mind

First and foremost, if his blowjob is part of your planned activities for the night, by all means wear something that flatters you. The old, ripped, and faded flannel nightgown should be put away for some cold night – you want your night to be *hot*! Colorful bra and panties, especially in red or black, a sheer nighty from Victoria's Secret, or even better, something really slutty from an online company, will make him start drooling even before you get his zipper open.

As you should know, high heels push up your bottom to "present" your readiness for mating and mounting – there is nothing sexier to a man than a scantily clad woman in heels turning her back on him. Set the lighting – candles are romantic, and they flatter a woman's appeal, unlike most harsh lighting.

Is his blow job going to occur somewhere else? Try "forgetting" a piece of underclothing to get him in the mood, knowing that you are extremely naughty and likely to do something dangerous, like blowing him in the front seat of his car. A skirt without panties will always catch a man's eye, as will a blouse sans bra when your nipples stiffen.

Move naturally and be feminine – you've got a bottom that he likes to watch move, so move it! Drop something and bend over to pick it up. He is looking at your ass, even if he pretends not to. There's nothing wrong with being clumsy, and accidentally flashing him. A man's eyes are drawn to a woman's breasts – just ask Madison Avenue. Is it your fault that you had a 'nip slip'?

Draw attention to your lips, and if it at all flatters your face, use a deep red lipstick or gloss, the more colorful and the wetter looking, the better. The lips and mouth are highly representative of your labia and pussy, and it never, ever hurts to remind him that you have those, too! If he sees that your mouth is moist, I guarantee you that he's going to be thinking about your wet pussy milliseconds later.

Don't ignore his other senses, though. A nice body spray, cologne or perfume, lightly applied, is appealing. Does he like the smell and taste of your pussy, and does cunnilingus turn him on (as it does many men)? A touch of the wetness at your pussy on the tip of your finger, artfully applied to his upper lip under the pretense of brushing off a crumb, will have his cock as hard as steel very quickly!

Small noises from the back of your throat, as though involuntary, turn a man on. You can't help but moan when you see him, right? All of these things contribute to predisposing your man to not only desire you, but opening him up to enjoying the ultimate act of pleasure and submission that you're going to bestow on your lover – sucking his cock.

Is there anything that appeals more to a man's visual sense, and his desire to dominate, than watching his woman suck his cock, and to see her look up at him with love and desire in her own eyes?

Ramping up His Desire

Would you like to have your man just ram his cock inside you without any foreplay, or would you rather that he stroke and caress you a bit beforehand? I'm going to go out on a limb and say the latter. Similarly, although men are much more anxious to get to the main event, and find it far easier to reach that stage than women, nonetheless, they will respond positively to their woman creating teasing anticipation just prior to fellatio.

One of the very best ways to add to the excitement your man is already feeling (after you primed him visually), is to give him the same tender, gentle caresses that you would appreciate. Not stroking the most sensitive, nerve ending rich areas like his cock head, frenulum, or foreskin, but rather the 'second-level' areas like his thighs, lower stomach, and his bottom (the cheeks, not his anus!)

These areas respond to touching, caressing, and massaging very positively, though they're not likely to lead to an orgasm by themselves. Stroking with the pads of your fingertips is very different from running the edges of your nails, leading to different sensations, but both are usually very welcome. Starting with the soft touch of the fingertip, and escalating by using the nails, with light pressure and increasing, sends a message of escalating excitement to your man. Remember that men respond very positively to a woman who herself gives off signs of sexual excitement.

You can also pinch lightly, and tug at hair in these areas to build excitement.

When Desire Overwhelms, He'll Plead For It!

From there, proceed to light stroking of the underside of his scrotum and light caressing or stroking of his shaft, your fingers just barely touching him there. By this point he's going to be very, very anxious to feel the moist heat of your mouth on his penis, particularly the very sensitive head, foreskin, and frenulum.

Don't immediately swallow his penis inside your mouth, if you want to continue teasing and building excitement. Rather, kiss the tip with its piss slit (that wetness you see there is probably pre-cum, as you've put him in the position where his penis really wants to explode.) You can lightly flick your tongue along the slit, and you'll probably hear a muffled groan – that means that you're doing it right!

You can continue with short licks, perhaps half the length of his shaft, sporadically and interspersed with kisses on the shaft, head, frenulum, and foreskin (which by this point is completely pulled back with the head exposed. Try to stroke upward as you lick, keeping the motion towards the head. This will go with his general sensation of things moving up and out, like his semen.

Remember that his orgasm is only going to last a few seconds, so the pleasure you give him here will add to his short burst of pleasure later and make him a bit more grateful for your consideration. He will be asking you to suck him, and whether you have mercy on him or continue teasing and building his excitement depends upon him and you. Men have a limited patience with teasing, though, so you may not want to drag it out too long.

Being a Loving Partner to an Erection in Need

Men have an expression for either failing to get an erection, or for one that collapses too quickly. They call it "Performance Anxiety." As the name implies, the owner of the erection is so concerned whether he will fail or not, that the thought becomes father to the deed, i.e., his anxiety about potentially failing causes him to actually fail.

There are many organic causes for this, but they call for medical diagnosis, and are beyond the scope of this guide. Here we're dealing with an otherwise able man who simply has psyched himself out of being the stud that you know he really is. You can be a helpful, loving partner and remove some of the conditions which may lead to potential failure.

Besides the problem not really being his fault (it's that fear that causes the failure, not he himself), it's not your fault either. It's perfectly natural, and wrong to wonder if *you're* the problem – perhaps not sexy enough, or didn't do things 'just right,' or you're not attractive enough – those are just *your* insecurities talking, don't fall into that trap! If you weren't perfect for each other, you wouldn't have gotten this far in the first place, right?

Sometimes people fall into the trap of trying to make a light joke to relax their partner at times like this, or to subconsciously express their anger at their partner's failure, but those responses not only make the immediate situation no better, but may also have long term consequences. And don't lash out at your man, it's just not worth it and it's certainly not constructive.

So, what *can* you do?

Indirect Sexual Attention

- **Talk to him**. Communication always makes a good relationship better. Let him know that you're not concerned about it. Let him open up to you (I know, men don't do that – often. But sometimes they do.) Talk about what excites him, and don't be judgmental, if it turns him on it might be something to try or at least keep in mind.

- **Set the mood**. Don't you think that candles make for a nice setting when you want to get in the mood? Well, the same is often true for your man – at least, when it's important to help him to relax. You don't need to overdo it, but several candles artfully placed can keep the attention off his insecurity, and on your mutual goal – getting him hard!

- **Oral attention – but not there.** Paying all of your attention to his penis might make him think that his hard cock is all that you're interested in. How about letting him know that the rest of him is important too, by kissing and tonguing him on his lips, and parts of his body that aren't supposed to be stiff and hard? Guys like kissing too!

- **Caresses and massages.** Any man can give himself an orgasm – they do it ALL THE TIME. But one thing he can't do, is to caress and massage himself, and most men ache for a woman's touch everywhere on his body. It is extremely relaxing to him to receive a massage on his back, or neck and shoulders, or anywhere else for that matter. He'll love the attention, and it really will take his mind off his cock.

- **Relax, yourself**. Your life doesn't depend on his erection this time. It's nice to cuddle and kiss, and you can let him know that you'll be ready for him whenever he's ready for you (even if you're not always.) That kind of stand-by-your-man confidence and patience goes a long way toward giving him confidence.

Direct Sexual Attention

- **Kissing and licking his cock from the start**. Cocks taste pretty good when they're soft, too, and you both get the marvelous sensation of feeling him get hard while he's in your mouth. You may not be able to 'deep throat' him when he's hard, but you probably can when he's not erect. Men love the thought that their woman is taking their whole thing in her mouth, it's especially slutty of you, but more importantly, shows him that you're not at all reluctant to suck his cock.

- **Go where the action is**. Remember that his most sensitive areas are the head of his cock, the frenulum on the underside of his cock, where the head meets the shaft, the foreskin, and to a lesser extent, the underside of his scrotum. Caressing, stroking, and softly and attentively kissing and licking those ultra-sensitive areas can pay off big time. Just because his penis isn't hard (for the moment,) doesn't mean that he's gone numb – in fact, mentally he's probably raring to go and desires your touch more than ever.

- **Everywhere else.** Mainly the shaft, though. When men masturbate, they usually stroke their shaft up and down, along with stroking the cock head itself, so that's the motion that they've trained their cock to respond to. You can benefit from that reflexive response by doing it too. Just be very careful that you handle that soft penis GENTLY – it's not a stick shift. I can't tell you the number of men who complain that their woman has a 'too-rough' touch on their cock, especially when it's soft. Take it easy!!

- **Sometimes it's a medical condition**. You can't solve every soft penis condition, sometimes it calls for medical consultation. Have you seen the ads for various 'blue pill' type solutions? If you both think that's the case, encourage your man to see a doctor – it's pretty simple these days for that kind of issue.

Oops, I told him to come, but he was already there - Dealing with premature ejaculation.

Dealing with premature ejaculation (PE) can seem very vexing to both partners, and it does require a little patience. There are three easy steps to helping your man deal with this issue: Edging, Hedging, and Kissing.

Edging. You probably don't want to begin a long conversation with him about PE, as that will focus his attention on the issue, which generally makes the problem worse. Instead of suggesting that you have a "cure" for him, suggest that you want to see if you both can learn to have multiple orgasms.

You need to bring him as close as you can to an orgasm, without going over the edge. This is a component of tantric sex – experiencing many low level orgasms in one pleasurable session. In order for this strategy to succeed, he needs to let you know when his orgasm is approaching. When he does, you pull back from your stimulation of his body, until the urge to ejaculate subsides.

Pretty soon, after following this course, he'll be feeling orgasms that are not as strong as the one orgasm he's used to, but together far exceed that pleasure. In the process, he'll learn to better control when he comes, and is done for the session, as well as becoming a much better partner for you in lovemaking.

Hedging. After you've worked on edging your man, then you'll be firmly squeezing the tube on the underside of his cock (urethra) between thumb and forefinger. Place fingers just below his cock head when applying pressure. This helps to prevent ejaculation.

Kissing. Return to the other aspects of lovemaking-- the pleasurable things that aren't directly related to a man's sexual stimulation, like kissing and caressing, holding each other, for at least one minute. That gives his cock the opportunity to cool down, but not so much that he loses interest. A big bonus – this will refocus him on your need to come, and as he's thinking more about your pleasure, he's also thinking less of his own, removing one of the causes of the anxiety which made him ejaculate prematurely in the first place.

Fellatio Techniques

There are three basic fellatio techniques available to any woman. These will have her pleasing her man with incredible stimulation, and are easily learned and applied.

Licking

Although your tongue by itself can't bring a man off, it has the ability to bring him to the heights of pleasure, using one of these two proven methods.

- **Tongue lashing** – Where are the most nerve endings on your man's entire body? Why, on the head of his cock, and his frenulum. If you lash him there with the tip of your tongue, the effect is much like that of having a tongue lashed over your clitoris – it's positively exciting! You can try this either while his cock head is between your lips, or you can do it without otherwise touching his body, a slow teasing touch of the tip of your tongue on the tip of his cock – enchanting!
- **Ice cream cone licking** – You know how to do this, pretend his great, big, delicious cock is a hot ice cream cone that's melting in your hand – goodness, you don't want to get a lapful of cream do you? Better swirl that hot, hungry, and wet tongue of yours up every side to collect his oozing, melting cream as it runs down the side!

Lips

Your tongue can't do all the work, and your lips are better equipped to handle the "heavy lifting" of giving your man a blow job. Lips have so much more area to contact your partner's hot, velvety, delicious rod, and are much softer than the surface of your tongue. The interplay of soft lips and rough tongue can drive a man insane with desire! Keep those lips wet, there's absolutely nothing wrong with actually drooling on his cock to keep the sensations so pleasant for him, and frankly, he'll be flattered to think that you find him mouth-watering!

- **Lip Kiss** – Remember where all those nerve endings are? A big, wet smacking kiss on his piss slit, with the contact of slick, wet lips smearing spit and pre-cum all over that plump cock head will remind him of how sweet your pussy feels when he just starts to enter you. Thinking of how wet and fun your pussy is, is sure to ensure that he's hard, and ready to fuck you.

- **Lip Tunnel** – Let his train enter your tunnel, by creating a sweet, wet and hot circular tunnel for his hot shaft to slip into, with your lips touching him all around on every part of his head, then the shaft, slipping down as far as you're able. You can use a soft touch (slight pressure) to help build his excitement towards climax, then a tighter grip (binding pressure) to over stimulate his nerve endings, and make him explode.
- **Lip Suck** – Apply a slight vacuum/sucking pressure with your lips on small areas of his penis, to give a different sensation than just simply contact.

Sucking

Unlike the lip sucking of the previous technique, this involves sucking larger areas. There are three basic areas that this can involve.

- **Ball sucking** – Your man will be absolutely stunned if you take either a part of his scrotum, or the "ball" itself inside the scrotum into your mouth, and lightly suck on it. This is a technique that is used by many gay men to get their lover off, and your man is likely to be just as thrilled, and just as hot to shoot, either *on* you or *in* you! Lightly grasp the shaft of his cock while you do this, both to lift his scrotum up so that you can get at it, and also to let him know that you didn't forget why you're down there. Remember that his balls are very sensitive to pain, so don't suck too hard, and don't twist anything down there. Lightly and gently, just as you'd like to be touched.
- **Head sucking** – swallow his entire cock head between your lips, and into your mouth, then gently suck on it. With thousands of nerve endings there, he's going to feel your suction, even if it's only slight. Remember that you can vary the suction, and that you can both move your mouth up and down as well as around the head, AND combine this with "Tongue lashing" and lightly stroking up and down the cock shaft with your fingers in a loose fist. This combination probably most often results in the man's cock erupting, hot

cum spurting out of his piss slit, than any other combination of techniques.

- **Shaft sucking** – Take as much of his head and shaft in your mouth as you comfortably can, seal your lips against the shaft, and suck while moving up and down with your lips, and if you like, swirling your tongue against his shaft and head, and applying softer or stronger suction. Because the shaft isn't as sensitive as the head, the physical excitement might not be as great as in "Head Sucking," but the emotional and visual kick that watching his woman so deeply and enthusiastically suck his dick gives him, is unparalleled for a man!

Ready to move on to some bonus techniques? Let's go!

8 Bonus Techniques

Heaven

The greatest technique to use in giving a blow job doesn't even involve his cock or the inside of your mouth! It's composed of four parts:

- **Eyes** – you've GOT to gaze lovingly or naughtily up at him while you're doing the deed. In interviews with men, every single one of them talked about what a power rush it is when their women looks up at them while she's sucking his dick, and the expression in her eyes seems to say that she's enjoying it – or at least getting off on both making her man happy, and being intimately connected to him.
- **Sounds** – moaning, cooing, even 'sloppy' sounds like sucking sounds, tell him that you're getting sexually excited by giving him head. Men don't want to think that a woman might not actually like having a penis in their mouth, and feel rejected if the fellatio is performed in a clinical, minimalist manner. So ham it up a little, and add sound effects!
- **Smile** – a smile says that having his cock in your mouth makes you happy, and making you happy makes him happy, especially when he doesn't have to go to a jewelry store! So, smile!
- **Combine** – always use several techniques together. Men are not excited if a girl only sucks, or strokes with her fingers, or licks, it makes them think that she's not really sure of how to give head. Oxymoronically, men want their women to be (or

seem to be) virginal, but they want her to fuck (or suck) like a whore!

Simple Simone

This may be the easiest technique of all. It's great when you're tired, and want to bring him off without killing yourself in the process. Simply place your mouth over the head of his cock, including his frenulum and at least part of his foreskin if he's uncircumcised, and swirl your tongue round the fringe of the head – that's the edges of the plump, velvety head. With two or three of your fingers and your thumb held in a loose circle, stroke up and down the shaft, from the base of his cock, up to your lips (which are only moving up and down a little.)

Many of my gay friends prefer this technique, because they can get their partner off more quickly this way. Remember, men are usually really more about the destination than the journey. They're usually not unhappy if you can bring them to an orgasm quickly.

Party Games

Maybe the most common physical party game is "Twister." When you twist your fingers as you stroke his shaft, or twist your lips around his cock head a little, or swirl your tongue around his cock head, then suddenly swirl in the other direction, you're adding another dimension to his blow job, and increasing his pleasure.

Nine to Three

Swirl your tongue across his cock head from side to side. Be sure to vary the cross movement frequently so that your tongue slides below the head, over the frenulum, because scraping your tongue again and again over his sensitive head can quickly become annoying to him.

Twelve to Six

Similarly, you can swirl your tongue up and down over the head, along (and even a little *into*) his piss slit, or urethra, licking up his pre-cum, and running right over his frenulum on the underside of his cock. Again vary the stroke of your tongue randomly to avoid irritating his penis.

Hillary

No, not that "Hillary," this is named after Edmund Hillary, who climbed Mt. Everest. Your tongue strokes up and down his hot, hard shaft, adding plenty of saliva along the way. Just as in your pussy, the more lube the better, so be free with it, and stroke your hot, wet tongue from the base of his cock all the way to the tip top, varying from side to side, top and undersides, etc.

Hurricane Emily

Named after a close friend of mine with whom I had a threesome. I watched in wonder as she wet our guy's cock head with her slurpy mouth, then blew on it, giving him the sensation of cool, then quickly swallowed his cock head in her warm mouth, in effect giving him a warm-cool-warm variation, again and again, until he quickly came.

I was a little annoyed, since he wasn't going to be fucking either of us after his massive eruption of come into her mouth, but when she used that same technique on my clit, I decided to forgive her!

The "Lovelace"

Named after adult film actress Linda Lovelace, who made the expression famous in the movie *Deep Throat*, this technique has you take your partner's erect cock deep inside your mouth so that his head is in the back of your mouth or even in your throat. The main impediment to carrying this off is the gag reflex. This is the reflex which causes you to vomit, or gag, when you stick your finger down your throat.

Some women lack this reflex, or have a poorly developed reflex, and taking a man's penis into their throat doesn't cause them any, or much, difficulty. Other women can train themselves to ignore this reflex, and can become very adept at sucking their partner's cock without gagging. Other women can never get past this reflex, but as there are many variations in both technique and position of cock sucking, they shouldn't feel that they're any sort of failure. This is an impressive technique, but it doesn't bring a man any extra pleasure that another technique can't match – it's more for bragging rights, his or yours!

I'd suggest that you try this technique once you're comfortable with taking a man's cock orally, taking it deeper and deeper over time. Practice with carrots, various sized dildos, etc. and you may surprise both yourself and your partner with your ability.

Because of the typical upward angle of a man's erect penis vis a vis his body (the "angle of the dangle" in common parlance), trying to take your partner's penis this way when you're kneeling before him will bring the head of his cock into your throat nerve endings and lead to subsequent failure. So, if you're facing his feet, or in a "69" position, his cock will be angled down into your throat. This position more easily avoids the gag reflex, increasing your likelihood of success. Again, practice makes perfect. If you try this position a few times during your fellatio sessions, you may well, over time, become expert at it and please your partner as few other women can.

"Accidental" Blow Jobs

Receiving a blow job from his female partner when he least expects it brings a man an unexpected pleasure, as well as positioning you as a partner who's not so predictable or stale in her lovemaking. Since it often involves locations other than the privacy of your home, caution is recommended, and practicing it when your partner is driving is definitely not safe! Here are some suggestions:

Anywhere around the house or yard – Of course, you need to have assurance of privacy, since everyone (including your neighbors) has a camera on their phone these days. But imagine how your partner's going to like it if you slide under his desk at home while he's telecommuting, slide down his pants, and give him a hot, wet, loving blow job? Not your typical work day, for sure! There are tons of locations that you might never have associated with sex before right there in your usual environment, which will bring him the ultimate pleasure.

"The kids were still asleep. There was some kind of teacher seminar thing going on, and when Terri walked me to the door to go to work, I didn't think too much about it. But when she looked into my eyes and began unzipping my suit trousers. I knew something was up. She reached her hand into my pants, then under my boxers, and loosely grasped my cock, lightly stroking up and down it, the whole time her eyes on mine, and an impish smile on her face.

I kind of melted, and started thinking about how I would lie to my boss about why I was late, because there was no way I was going to turn down sex with my wife. With two young kids, we don't do it often enough. Terri got up on tiptoes, and kissed my ear, then whispered in it.

'I saw you window shopping at the sports store,' she whispered. Her soft, warm breath racing over my ear, tickling a little, and I knew that she was setting up a fantasy situation for us. She giggled.

'I get so bored selling pretzels all day from that cart, mister, and when I saw that hot ass of yours I wanted to have lunch early, you know what I mean?'

Getting into her fantasy, I said. 'Yeah, I get you. What's your name, miss?'

'I'm Tammy,' Teri said, giggling again. Her scenario was spinning out of her control, and she loved it. 'I'm a freshman in college and I work here part time.'

'Well, Tammy, let's check out this photo booth, and maybe we can get some picture to remember our time together,' *I said in as dirty a tone as I could manage. Terri giggled again.*

'Okay, but you're gonna have to put in the 5 bucks for the machine,' she said, her eyes devilish. The 'photo machine' looked a lot like the overstuffed chair by the sofa in our living room, but we were both heavily into our roles – me, the random guy in the mall, her, the slutty teenager.

Terri, or 'Tammy,' pushed me down into the chair, and yanked my trousers down to my knees, freeing my cock, which sprung up pointing at midnight and as hard as I could ever remember it being.

'Oh my, that's so BIG,' *Tammy whined.*

'Suck it,' I growled. She brought her face down to my cock, and I could already see a little bubble of cum filling the piss slit at the top. I hoped that I wouldn't cum too fast, because Terri had gotten me so hot, but I wanted her to get a chance to cum, too. She began sucking my cock, and if I didn't know how much she loves me, I'd be suspicious that she'd been practicing on some other guy. She was not giving me the dead fish blow job that I'd gotten used to.

She was looking up at me with this 'fuck me' look in her eyes, and her lips and tongue and mouth were like nothing I'd ever felt before, the way she moved. Then her little hand, so soft and warm, was stroking up and down my cock. It was just fantastic.

Well, I wish I could tell you that she somehow kept me hot and hard for hours, but honestly, I shot off in her mouth pretty quickly, just barely getting out a warning that I was going to cum. She surprised the crap out of me then. Instead of jerking my cock out of her mouth and making a look, she just looked up at me as though she was thinking, 'I love this!' and kept sucking.

I was wondering if there was gonna be an argument about my sperm later, but when that urge hit me, I said 'fuck it' to myself, thrust my hips and jammed my dick as far into her mouth as I could. Terri, or Tammy, I guess, looked a little startled, but she hung on, keeping my cock in her mouth as I jetted my jizz inside her. God, I felt such intense love for her at that moment!

She swallowed my whole load, something she'd never done before, not even when we were dating. Then she slowly let my dick slip out of her mouth after I'd softened, licked her lips and smiled up at me, and said, 'That was better than an ice cream cone, mister.'

And then she got up off her knees, and walked into the kitchen. I sat there a few minutes, wondering what just happened, but finally zipped up and went off to work. I called her during the day, a couple of times, something that I hadn't done in years, and we had sex that night, and I went down on Terri, which I used to like, but hadn't done in a long time. She tasted every bit as good as I remembered, and I wondered why I'd stopped eating her pussy. She came a bunch of times, and we both slept really, REALLY well for a change.

I'm thinking that maybe we reinvest a little bit more of our time in each other from now on." – Kevin, 39

9 "Not Your Usual Location" Blow Jobs

While Showering

Men are always open to having their woman give them a blow job while in the shower, and you can be assured he's nice and clean while you do it!

In The Water

Whether in the bath tub, hot tub, or swimming pool, these are great locations for oral sex. Hotel rooms with Jacuzzis are usually only a few dollars more, so while you're traveling spend a few extra dollars and give him a Jacuzzi blow job, then you can both relax in the soothing bubbles. Don't be surprised if he "surprises" you a few hours later with some hot, kinky sex in, on, or under the bed!

Larger Bodies of Water

A leisurely float on a lake becomes a hot session of sex for you both when you float off to your own private cove, out of sight of others, and you take his cock in your mouth, using the techniques you've learned here. He'll be thrilled, and likely won't take long to come in excitement.

Don't forget "On the Beach." I refuse to have vaginal sex anywhere near sand, but I'll happily get on my knees to give the right man a blow job in a tropical beach setting!

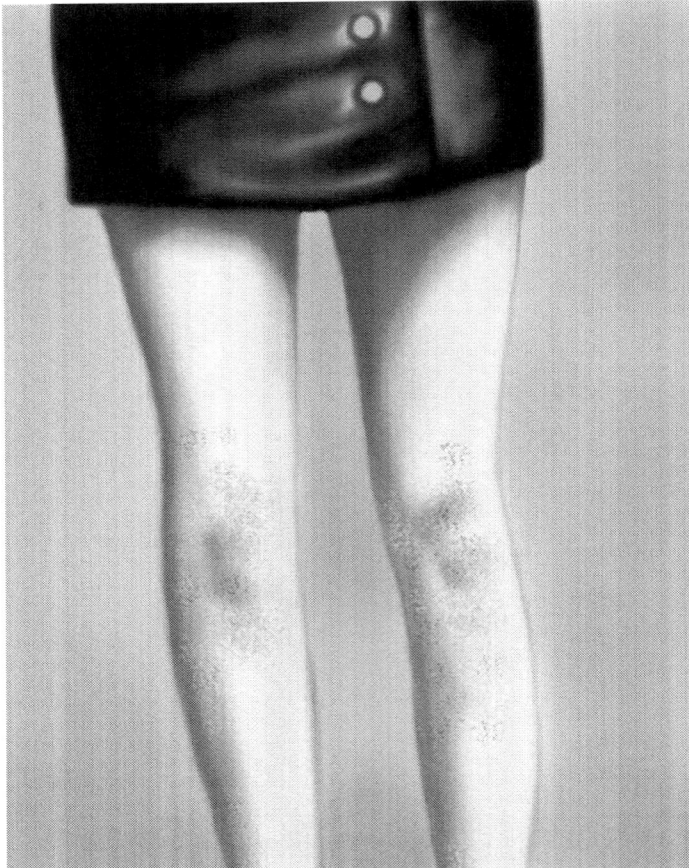

Public Transport

Okay, this is wildly exciting because there are bound to be other people nearby, but with discretion and a little common sense, you may be able to pull it off.

- **Airplanes** - On an airplane, you'll want to choose a sparsely filled, 'red eye' flight in the wee hours, when even the flight attendants have disappeared, and you definitely want to use a blanket, coat, or other concealments to hide what's going on! And if the pilot has ordered everyone, including flight attendants to remain seated, great, but watch those sudden drops in altitude.

- **Long Bus Trips** – The possibility of this may be enough to make you ride a long distance carrier even if you never did before. Since the only official around is the driver, and he's busy driving, the same airplane scenario has a greater chance of success and less risk of discovery on a bus. This probably won't work on your typical city bus, so confine this to longer trips!
- **Ferry Rides** – The Staten Island Ferry and the Puget Sound ferries can provide some of the most memorable settings for romantic blow jobs, and also the time necessary them. Many other states operate ferries in equally exciting settings, with opportunities for the daring and adventurous. In the car? Out of the car? That depends on your discovery danger threshold!

Campout at Home

Have you got a yard of any size? Combine that with some pleasant weather, blankets, sleeping bags or tents optional, and you have some of the most romantic environments possible in which to please your partner orally.

In the Wild

Well, not TOO wild. But you may have tons of meadows, forests, or even scrub brush like that found along seashores, where you can find a small cozy secluded haven for two, just you and your partner, and his cum-filled cock – not to mention his eternal gratitude for a mind blowing sexual experience!

"It was idyllic, really. Bret planned the whole thing and found a meadow full of beautiful blue wildflowers, and even remembered to bring a blanket for us to lie on. I never had so much fun sucking his cock, and I felt very special." – Liz, 18

Abandoned structures

Old, abandoned houses and factory buildings that are overgrown by vegetation (and not used by crack addicts or as meth labs!) are scenic, beautiful locations for some al fresco oral sex, as your partner leans back on a wall with one hundred year old faded wallpaper, and you rest on your knees pleasing him.

Road Head

Please, do this while you're parked. The excitement from the slight chance you might get caught, and the pleasure of being serviced by his partner in the familiar location, adds spice to any blow job. Don't bang your head on the steering wheel!

Public Restrooms

Some of the best oral sex happens in these places every day. One person type restrooms are perfect for this, as they can be locked, and obviously have more privacy than multiple person restrooms. Of course, commandeering a stall in a multi-person men's or ladies room is not unheard of, but if you're too noisy or take a needed stall out of commission for too long, irate patrons may notify the people in charge or even police.

Other Sites

Laundromats late at night, playgrounds after hours, even amateur, high school, college, and professional sports fields at late night have been used for impromptu oral sex sessions, though we can't attest to the wisdom or safety of these sites!

15 Fellatio Positions

Oral Traditional

In this position, he'll be on his back, with his cock pointing toward the ceiling (or sky.) Everyone uses this position, so it's got tradition and numbers going for it. You'll be facing downward, on your stomach or humped up a bit on your knees, between his legs. Of course, you're facing his cock, and beyond that, you're looking in his eyes if he gets up on his elbows. If you do it right, he gets to watch you sucking his cock, with your eyes meeting his. If you've by chance gotten up on your knees, with your ass in the air, he also gets to look at your back and especially, your sweet ass. That ought to keep his erection going!

Oral Nuevo

Similar to **Oral Traditional**, the difference is that he's almost sitting up. In this position, he can see all of your body, from head to feet, as you enthusiastically and passionately tongue his pole. It's also a bit easier for you to bring in your hands on his cock shaft and scrotum, along with all of the pleasure that your lips, tongue, and mouth are bringing to his sex. With the added visual stimulus, and better use of your hands in this position, he'll have trouble holding off that orgasm, and spraying you (where you want) with his hot, sticky cum.

Submissive Sweetheart

Oh wow, men absolutely LOVE this position! It fulfills the excitement of every dirty movie blow job they've ever seen. Don't be surprised when he gets a little rough with you, pulling your hair and absolutely calling you a filthy slut (in a good way, of course.)

He is standing, looking down at you, as you kneel before him, your eyes adoringly on his cute prick as it flexes and bounces with his nervous tension. You are on your knees, so make sure that you're kneeling on something soft and thick, or that hard floor is going to HURT. You submissively look up at him as you mouth his hard dick, and he'll likely alternate between cooing to you, and treating you like the slut that you want to be as his excitement rises. Orgasms usually come pretty fast with this position!

"Steven wanted me to kneel in front of him and give him a blow job, instead of us just laying on the bed. He got really wild, pulling my hair, calling me a 'slut,' just acting like he really got into it, which had never happened with the other times on the bed. Instead of coming, though, he actually threw me on the bed and fucked into me (not my ass!) from behind harder and deeper than I could ever remember. Best of all, nine months later, we had little Jennifer! So, yes, I like doing it that way." – Heather, 23

Spiced Rum

This is a whimsical variation of **Submissive Sweetheart.** Instead of standing flat footed, he should have one foot up a foot or so off the floor, like the namesake of a certain popular spiced rum.

Caribbean Vacation

He's sitting in a comfortable chair (I always picture one of those rattan or wicker fan back chairs that you find in tropical locales, hence the name of the position.) You're kneeling, or sitting between his legs, depending upon the height of his seat. Of course it's HIS Caribbean Vacation, not yours – you're the serving girl or native girl cleaning his room, whose duties and pleasures include sucking the master's hot and ready cock while he relaxes and lets you do all the work.

The Pussycat

Meow! Picture two cats approaching each other, one male, one female. After a brief nose nuzzle, the male rises up and fucks his cock into the female's hot and wet mouth, as she remains on all fours. Every guy loves this, he kneels as you suck his cock, and he can thrust with his hips, literally fucking your mouth. What's not to like?

Whistle While You Work

You are sitting, while he stands, doing whatever it is he's doing, like writing some super important man document by hand. His hard, erect cock beckons to you with its rosy, hot anger and his wet piss slit, so you lean forward while he's standing, and slide your lips around that big, delicious lollipop...

Soixante-neuf

Popularly known as "69," this is the most sharing of all the positions, because there's actually some physical stimulation in it for you, too. The drawback is that, if you do it right, neither of you can focus quite as well as you could if it were just one partner pleasuring the other. Oh well, that's the price you pay for mutual orgasms, I guess.

Unless you and he are similarly sized, if he's at all bigger than you, HE MUST BE ON THE BOTTOM. I can't emphasize this strongly enough. Having a big guy fall on you from a height after coming can be distressing. Take it from me, I KNOW.

Passing Trains

This is an easy variation of **Soixante-neuf**, with both of you on your sides, orally pleasuring each other.

Ten 'til Noon

With him lying on his back, you're at an angle to his body, and on your stomach, with your feet at the 10 o'clock position and his head at the 12 o'clock position, and his feet more or less at 6 o'clock, so that you're partially straddled across his body, and he can look closely at some of the very interesting parts of your body, stroking and caressing you as you suck his cock. Remember, one of his greatest turn-ons is just looking at your delectably delish body!

Trapéziste

Or, French for "Trapeze Artist."As you lie on your back on the bed, head hanging over the edge backward and down, he walks up to you and slowly and gently inserts his cock into your mouth, pressing deeper and deeper, and because of the angle, your throat may never realize that it's being fucked by a man's cock – and you've just given him your first Lovelace!

Pearl Necklace

Yes, this is the one that ZZ Top was singing about, and according to lead singer Billy Gibbons, "it really don't cost that much." You're lying on your back, he's straddling your upper body with his legs as he kneels above you, his cock dangerously close to your mouth, but also within striking distance of your breasts.

Even if you don't have humongous boobs for him to fuck between, he can still jack himself off while rubbing against your tits, the head of his cock slipping in and out of your wet, hot mouth. It won't take him long, as dicks and tits are an explosive combination for some reason. When he cums, let that good goo fly wherever you all agreed, whether in your mouth for you to happily swallow, on your breasts, or on your throat for that legendary 'pearl necklace.'

The Zipper

In this position, you're lying on your back, and he's above you, facing you, as though he were going to fuck your pussy in the missionary position, only... he's going to fuck your mouth instead, so he moves up about two or three feet so that his cock is going to plunge down, hard, into your wet and willing mouth. Another position popular with guys, though he has to be in decent physical condition to support himself above you.

Fireman's Carry

I don't know if firemen actually quite carry people around like this, but many of us would be happy if they did! Face each other on your sides, but with him further up your body as in **The Zipper**. You can hump his leg with your oozing wet pussy while he watches you sucking his cock. That's fun for everybody!

S.O.M.F

This stands for "Sit On My Face." You're lying on your back, with your male partner squatting over your breasts, bringing his cock downwards to your mouth, and letting you do your thing on him. It's a closer to your face variation of **Pearl Necklace**, with a different angle and strictly mouth and finger stimulus, rather than using your breasts to excite him. You'll want a "safe gesture" to use if he gets carried away, and you can't breathe. Make sure he's clear on what it is, and what it means.

Eating Down Under - The Art and Skill of the Swallow

From a man's perspective, the second worst thing that can happen (besides a poorly performed blow job), is a poorly received blow job ejaculation. Fellatio, in most cases, is a two person act (there are guys that can actually blow themselves, but that's another story.) Does he end up enjoying it? Does she?

You have to decide whether you want to make his satisfaction paramount when you perform fellatio, or are you just going to do a half-assed blow job "because he wants it"? Since you're reading this guide, I believe that – regardless of how you feel about taking a man's penis in your mouth - you really want *him* to enjoy it. And that's only fair, right? When he licks your clit and pussy, you should be able to expect that he will bring you to orgasm.

So anyway, men have no difficulty whatsoever figuring out when you don't "like" his semen, the physical expression of his orgasm. Maybe your first blow job as a teenager was a shock to you, maybe you had an abusive boyfriend who forced you to swallow, whatever the reason, if you're carrying emotional baggage regarding the conclusion of fellatio, you are ruining the event for your man.

What to do?

The main problem with semen, as I see it, is the consistency. It's kind of weird, and I won't go into what it compares to, but the slick, slippery feel, and the sometimes odd taste and smell, can turn women off. But really, it's hardly the worst thing that's ever gone in your mouth or stomach, if you're honest with yourself. Remember, a man

57

takes a chance every time he sticks his face between a woman's thighs, so both sexes do face a few challenges in that arena.

Men generally feel disappointed with the blow job if it concludes with his partner:

- Making a face
- Making some negative comment about the taste, smell, feel, or generally
- Spitting the semen out
- Unexpectedly jerking his penis out of her mouth and his semen going god knows where

All or any of the above are often taken as signs of rejection of the man himself by his partner. How would you feel if he kicked you out of bed right after you came (assuming you DID come!) You'd feel bad, right – lovemaking isn't finished until you're reaffirmed by his holding you. His lovemaking is finished a lot earlier, but *after* his semen comes flying out of the head of his penis. So, do yourself a GIANT favor, finish the "job" correctly, and he will love your ability to give him head.

Where Should His Semen Go, and How Can You Make Him Happy?

Believe it or not, not every man has to have you swallow his ejaculate to be happy. Communicate with him to see what he wants. Some men have to see you swallow his semen every time – in my opinion, they're rather insecure. Other men would like you to swallow sometimes – again, a little insecure, but pretty normal. And some men don't care at all, they just want to get their rocks off – they're certainly the easiest to please!

My position on this subject is, you're supposed to be bringing him to the greatest orgasm of his life, so you should be doing whatever it takes to make him happy. Try to clear your mind of past unpleasantness with blow jobs, and concentrate on *his* happiness.

Communicate – you've both got to be clear what the limits are on the endpoint of his orgasm. If you're not going to swallow it, or take it in your mouth, by all means, nicely let him know that. If you don't both agree beforehand, he's going to take it as your rejection of him, even though presumably that's not your intent at all. And once his ejaculation starts, he's not in any position to hold it off while you both dither over disposal.

So, let him know beforehand that it's going into a tissue or towel after it goes in your mouth, or that you'll be happy to take a shot to the face (close your eyes!), or onto your breasts, or, if you're adept, onto your ass (which men seem to love.) And of course, best case scenario for him is to watch his jizz jet into your mouth, and see your tongue licking up a stray droplet off your lips, then gulp ostentatiously and smile as his creamy, hot come slides down your throat.

If you *do* swallow his load, it's only fair that he agrees to kiss you afterwards. If he balks, then you've got the leverage to justify not swallowing or taking it in the mouth. Men are extremely flattered when a woman swallows his come, so do keep that in mind. If you don't mind doing it, it's an easy way to score points.

However you handle the product of his bliss, have him aware that it is his responsibility to warn you when he feels orgasm approaching, so that you can take care of business properly. Men appreciate if you make some sort of "happy sound" when he comes, otherwise it's as though his "gift" to you is falling flat. Moans, soft sighs, even filthy talk *("oh god, yesss, give me your hot cum!")* make him feel unbelievably good about how involved you are in his pleasure.

If you want to know how I feel about the whole subject, I'm all for swallowing his come, and making as big a show about it as I can, because it costs me so little, and it makes him feel so good. Obviously, though, every woman has to choose for herself. Just try not to let a bad first experience turn you off forever to what can be a wonderful sharing between the two of you.

Solving the Peskiest Fellatio Problem

We've talked about Premature Ejaculation, and erection problems, and how to solve them – so what is the *peskiest, most annoying* problem?

Simple, he just can't come, even though you're breaking your jaw to give him your best oral. So, what to do?

The easiest way for a man to come, is generally at his own hand. Men masturbate thousands of times in their lives – they know better than anyone how to make themselves come. Let your man stroke his cock, while you loosely mouth just the head. The combination of his familiar stroking, along with the implicit promise of shooting his hot load in your wet and willing mouth, is irresistible to almost any man. Before you know it, he'll be groaning with pleasure, and his jizz will be, well, wherever you two agreed it should go!

Keeping Medical Risks in Mind

Regardless of what any past United States Presidents may say or think, oral sex presents the possibility of transmission of sexually transmitted diseases (STD), and precautions should be taken.

If you're monogamous, in a committed relationship, then generally continued testing for STDs is not necessary. If you're sexually active and not in a monogamous relationship, then you really should be practicing safer fellatio. As the partner receiving ejaculate, you are more at risk than your partner, so it's important for the protection of your health that you are aware of potential risks.

Here are three sites that you can use to learn more about STDs and fellatio:

http://en.wikipedia.org/wiki/Sexually_transmitted_disease

http://std.about.com/od/prevention/ht/safefellatio.htm

http://www.uhs.uga.edu/sexualhealth/oral_sex.html

And this site is a little "tongue in cheek," but it's fun and does have useful information:

www.dontspitswallow.com

As the "giving" (but really "receiving") partner in oral sex with a male, you should be aware of the possible infection risks involved from these STDs:

- HIV
- Hepatitis A, B, C
- Genital and Oral Herpes

- Human Papillomavirus (genital warts)
- Syphilis
- Gonorrhea
- Chlamydia

It's in your best interests to protect yourself, whatever form of sexual intercourse you choose. So, educate yourself and stay safe!

Books by Melinda Holmes

Blow Her Mind

50 Shades of Better Sex

Blow His Mind

www.amazon.com/author/melindaholmes

About Melinda Holmes

Melinda Holmes is the author of numerous award winning fiction and non-fiction erotic stories and books. She writes about the relationship issues of sex and love that tantalize and excite men and women throughout the English speaking world. Her fans number in the millions, and can be found in all levels of society. Her breezy, light and easy take on the pleasurable battles of sexual combat charm thousands of readers daily.

A 1990s graduate of a religious college in the State of California in the United States, Holmes has come a long way from her restrictive upbringing to blast apart the strictures and bonds that prevent lovers from reaching their greatest sexual potential. Her writing, both humorous and hot, will leave you laughing even as you find your libido buzzing.

She has made numerous friendships in the erotic entertainment community, as well as intimate relationships with many of the men and women there, giving her unique insight into successful methods of achieving the pleasurable heights that each of us deserves.

Besides the plaudits of her many fans, her achievements in related fields include training in interpersonal relationships, marriage and relationship counseling, the psychology of fetish sex, and many professional writing awards. Her writing displays the insight, wisdom, experience, scholarship and most importantly, the innate sense of fun that make her works hard to put down and an entertainment whirlwind that you'll be telling all of your friends about!

Exclusive Bonus Download: 101 Steps To A Happy Relationship

Download your bonus, please visit the download link above from your PC or MAC. To open PDF files, visit http://get.adobe.com/reader/ to download the reader if it's not already installed on your PC or Mac. To open ZIP files, you may need to download WinZip from http://www.winzip.com. This download is for PC or Mac ONLY and might not be downloadable to kindle.

Dating and marriage is different today than it was twenty years ago. In today's society, more than 50% of all marriages fail for one reason or another. Just thinking about that makes "commitment" seem scary. It seems that when relationships are faced with challenges, people quit trying.

The fact is that relationships, whether dating or married, are hard. Things do not always go perfectly, fighting does occur, and it takes a 100% commitment from both parties to make it a success.

There are hundreds of things you can do to better your relationship. To help get you headed in the right direction, 101 Steps To A Happy Relationship

Visit the URL above to download this guide and start improving your relationship NOW

One Last Thing...

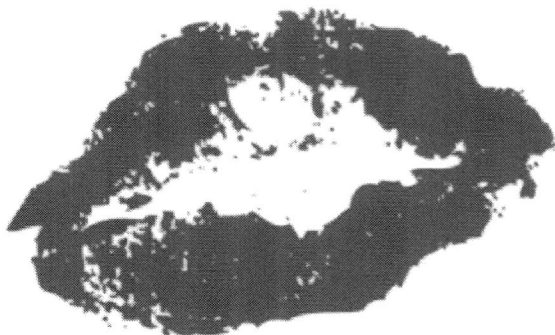

Thank you so much for reading my book. I hope you really liked it. As you probably know, many people look at the reviews on Amazon before they decide to purchase a book. If you liked the book, could you please take a minute to leave a review with your feedback? 60 seconds is all I'm asking for, and it would mean the world to me.

Melinda Holmes

Images and Cover by Sensual Science Publishing

Sensual
Science
PUBLISHING

Atlanta, Georgia USA

34025500R00045

Made in the USA
Lexington, KY
19 July 2014